MLB's Greatest Teams

HOUSTON ASTROS

Big Buddy Books

An Imprint of Abdo Publishing
abdobooks.com

Caroline Wesley

abdobooks.com

Published by Abdo Publishing, a division of ABDO, PO Box 398166, Minneapolis, Minnesota 55439.
Copyright © 2019 by Abdo Consulting Group, Inc. International copyrights reserved in all countries. No part
of this book may be reproduced in any form without written permission from the publisher. Big Buddy Books™
is a trademark and logo of Abdo Publishing.

Printed in the United States of America, North Mankato, Minnesota.
102018
012019

Cover Photo: Christian Petersen/Getty Images.
Interior Photos: 33ft/Depositphotos (p. 7); Bob Levey/Getty Images (p. 9); Bud Symes/Getty Images (p. 13);
    Christian Petersen/Getty Images (pp. 17, 21); Cliff Welch/AP Images (p. 22); Craig Melvin/Getty Images
    (p. 23); Ed Kolenovsky/AP Images (p. 11); Elsa/Getty Images (p. 19); Ezra Shaw/Getty Images (p. 29);
    Kevork Djansezian/Getty Images (p. 27); RH/AP Images (p. 22); Ronald Martinez/Getty Images (p. 5);
    Stephen Dunn/Getty Images (p. 28); Streeter Lecka/Getty Images (pp. 24, 25); Thearon W. Henderson/
    Getty Images (p. 15).

Coordinating Series Editor: Tamara L. Britton
Contributing Editor: Jill M. Roesler
Graphic Design: Jenny Christensen, Cody Laberda

Library of Congress Control Number: 2018948453

Publisher's Cataloging-in-Publication Data

Names: Wesley, Caroline, author.
Title: Houston Astros / by Caroline Wesley.
Description: Minneapolis, Minnesota : Abdo Publishing, 2019 | Series: MLB's
    greatest teams set 2 | Includes online resources and index.
Identifiers: ISBN 9781532118081 (lib. bdg.) | ISBN 9781532171123 (ebook)
Subjects: LCSH: Houston Astros (Baseball team)--Juvenile literature. | Baseball
    teams--United States--History--Juvenile literature. | Major League Baseball
    (Organization)--Juvenile literature. | Baseball--Juvenile literature.
Classification: DDC 796.35764--dc23

Contents

Major League Baseball

League Play

There are two leagues in MLB. They are the American League (AL) and the National League (NL). Each league has 15 teams and is split into three divisions. They are east, central, and west.

The Houston Astros is one of 30 Major League Baseball (MLB) teams. The team plays in the American League West **Division**.

Throughout the season, all MLB teams play 162 games. The season begins in April and can continue until November.

Orbit is the team's mascot. In 2018, Orbit released a children's book called *Orbit's First Day of School*!

A Winning Team

The Astros team is from Houston, Texas. The team's colors are navy blue, orange, and light orange.

The team has had good seasons and bad. But time and again, the Astros players have proven themselves. Let's see what makes the Astros one of MLB's greatest teams!

Fast Facts

HOME FIELD: Minute Maid Park

TEAM COLORS: Navy blue, orange, and light orange

TEAM SONG: "Go, Go Astros" by Mack Hayes

PENNANTS: 2

WORLD SERIES TITLES: 2017

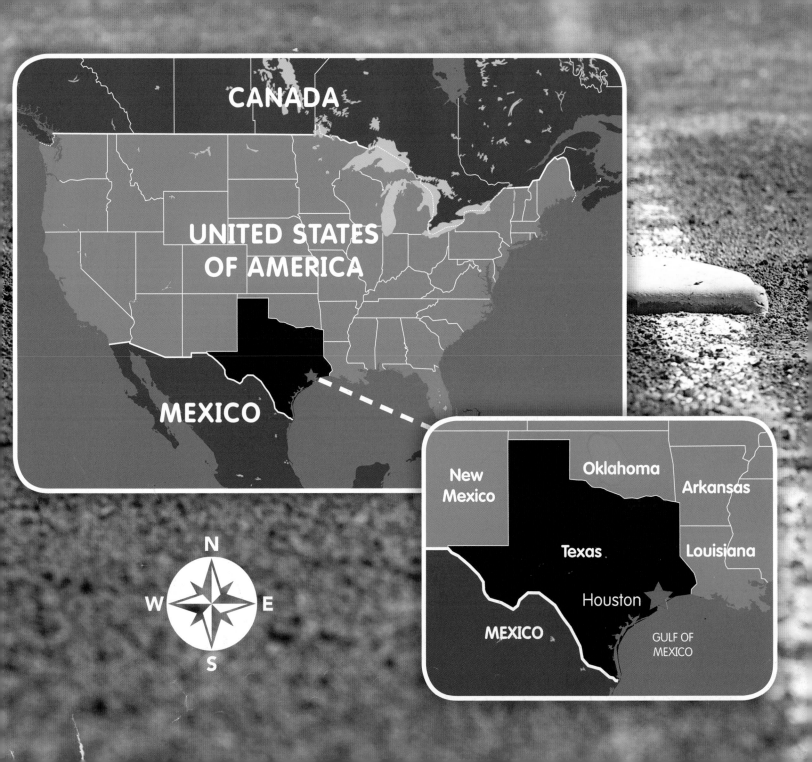

Minute Maid Park

The Astros began playing in Colt Stadium in 1962. After only three years, the team moved to the Astrodome. It was the first stadium to use a fake grass called AstroTurf.

The new Astros stadium opened in downtown Houston in 2000. It was first called Enron Field. But the name changed to Astros Field in 2002.

That same year, the field was renamed to Minute Maid Park. The stadium holds more than 40,000 fans.

The Astros play against four other teams in the West Division. They are the Los Angeles Angels, the Oakland Athletics, the Seattle Mariners, and the Texas Rangers.

Then and Now

The Astros team began in 1962 when the NL added two more teams to its league. Houston received one of the new teams. It was named the Houston Colt .45s.

Three years later, the name changed to the Houston Astros. The Astros played in the NL for 51 years. Then in 2013, the team joined the AL West **Division**.

The Astrodome was the first MLB stadium with a domed roof.

The Astros had only three winning seasons during the 1970s. But players began to have better luck in the early 1980s. In 1980, they went to the **playoffs**. There, they won the **Division** Series for the first time.

Sadly, the Astros lost to the Philadelphia Phillies in the **Championship** Series. But the players went back to the playoffs in 1981 and 1986. The team continued to place near the middle of the division throughout the late 1980s and early 1990s.

Astros was a perfect name for the team. Houston is home to NASA's Johnson Space Center.

Highlights

From 1990 to 2010, the Astros had 14 winning seasons. During this time, the team made it to the **playoffs** six times.

In 2004, the Astros made it to the playoffs as a **wild-card** team. The team won the NL **Division** Series, but not the **Championship** Series.

The following year, the Astros made it all the way to the World Series. Sadly, the team lost to the Chicago White Sox.

In his first year with the Astros, Evan Gattis hit 11 triples but never stole a base. This is a feat accomplished by only two other players in MLB history.

Win or Go Home

The top team from each AL and NL division goes to the playoffs. Each league also sends one wild-card team. One team from the AL and one from the NL will win the pennant. The two pennant winners then go to the World Series!

The Astros were **determined** to play in the World Series again. So the team added more talented players to its **roster**.

In 2017, the Astros won its first AL **division** title. Then the players beat the New York Yankees in the AL **Championship** Series.

Finally, the Astros advanced to the World Series. The team beat the Los Angeles Dodgers five to one in Game Seven. This win marked the Astros' first World Series title!

Outfielder George Springer won the World Series Most Valuable Player (MVP) Award in 2017.

Famous Managers

Larry Dierker began his MLB **career** at age 17 pitching for the Colt .45s. He continued to pitch for the Astros from 1965 to 1976.

Dierker went on to manage the team from 1997 to 2001. Under his management, the Astros made it to the **playoffs** four times. To honor Dierker, the Astros **retired** his jersey number 49 in 2002.

In 1998, Dierker *(left)* led the team to 102 wins. That was the most wins in Astros history.

A past MLB catcher, AJ Hinch joined the Astros in 2015. He was **nominated** for 2015 AL Manager of the Year in his first year.

Hinch led the Astros to 101 wins in 2017. These wins brought the team to its first World Series victory. Because of the team's success, Hinch was considered one of the best MLB managers of his time.

Hinch won the Baseball America Manager of the Year Award after the 2017 World Series win.

Star Players

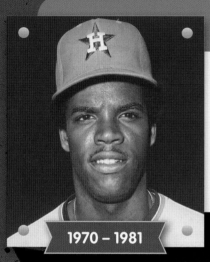

1970 – 1981

César Cedeño OUTFIELDER, #28

César Cedeño is one of the best outfielders in Astros' history. In 12 seasons, he **putout** more than 3,300 batters. He earned five **Gold Glove Awards** for his skills in the field. As a batter, Cedeño hit 163 home runs. And he had nearly 500 **stolen bases** while with the team.

Nolan Ryan PITCHER, #34

Nolan Ryan is one of MLB's greatest pitchers. In only nine years, he **struck out** nearly 2,000 batters! He earned two NL pitching titles for his talent on the mound. In 1980, Ryan became the first MLB player to earn $1 million a season.

1980 – 1988

Craig Biggio SECOND BASEMAN, #7

Craig Biggio became part of the Astros in 1988. Together, he and teammate Jeff Bagwell were called "the Killer B's." The two had many strong plays on the field. Biggio won five **Silver Slugger Awards** for batting. He also won four **Gold Glove Awards** for his fielding skills. He joined the National Baseball Hall of Fame in 2015.

1988 – 2007

Jeff Bagwell FIRST BASEMAN, #5

1991 – 2005

Throughout his **career** with the Astros, Jeff Bagwell won many awards. In his first year, he won the 1991 NL **Rookie** of the Year Award. He also earned an NL **MVP** Award, a Gold Glove Award, and three Silver Sluggers. In 2017, he was named to the National Baseball Hall of Fame.

23

José Altuve SECOND BASEMAN, #27

José Altuve began playing in the minor leagues as a teenager. At 21, he joined the Astros. During the 2017 **playoffs**, Altuve hit two home runs. This helped the Astros win its first World Series! That same year, he earned the AL Hank Aaron Award for best hitter in the league. Altuve also won the AL **MVP** Award in 2017.

2011 –

Dallas Keuchel PITCHER, #60

The Astros **drafted** Dallas Keuchel in 2009. The left-handed pitcher played his first MLB game in 2012. For his pitching excellence, Keuchel won three **Gold Glove Awards** in a row. In 2015, Keuchel won The Sporting News' AL Pitcher of the Year Award. That year he also earned his first Cy Young Award.

2012 –

George Springer OUTFIELDER, #4

George Springer was selected as a first-round **draft** pick for the Astros in 2011. As a **rookie**, Springer hit 20 homers in his first season. For his efforts, he earned the May 2014 Rookie of the Month Award. Later, he won the 2017 World Series **MVP** Award. He won the award after hitting five home runs in seven World Series games.

2014 –

Carlos Correa SHORTSTOP, #1

Carlos Correa was the first pick in the 2012 MLB draft. Three years later, he began playing for the Astros. In his first season with the team, Correa won AL Rookie of the Year. And in 2017, he earned the AL Player of the Month Award. Correa played in one All-Star Game and in the World Baseball Classic.

2015 –

Final Call

The Houston Astros have a long, rich history. The team has played in two World Series, and earned one World Series title.

Even during losing seasons, true fans have stuck by the players. Many believe the Astros will remain one of the greatest teams in MLB.

All-Stars

The best players from both leagues together each year for All-Star Game. This game count toward the regular records. It is simply celebrate the best players in MLB.

The Astros won the 2018 ESPY Award for Best Team. Players *(from left)* Dallas Keuchel, José Altuve, and Alex Bregman accepted the award onstage.

Through the Years

1960

The Astros were one of two new teams to join the NL.

1972 – 1974

César Cedeño stole more than 50 bases and hit more than 20 home runs for three straight seasons. He was the first player in history to do so.

1981

MLB players stopped playing for nearly two months. More than 700 games were cancelled throughout MLB! But the Astros still made it to the **playoffs**.

1986

The Astros played in the NL **Championship** Series. Game Six lasted 16 **innings**.

1994

Jeff Bagwell became the first Astros player to win the NL **MVP** Award.

2000

The team played its first game at the new Enron Field. More than 3 million fans attended Astros games that season!

2005

The Astros played the Chicago White Sox in the longest World Series game. Game Three lasted five hours and 41 minutes.

2017

The Astros won its first World Series in seven games against the Los Angeles Dodgers!

Glossary

career a period of time spent in a certain job.

championship a game, a match, or a race held to find a first-place winner.

determined free from doubt about doing something.

division a number of teams grouped together in a sport for competitive purposes.

draft a system for professional sports teams to choose new players.

Gold Glove Award annually given to the MLB players with the best fielding experience.

inning a division of a baseball game that consists of a turn at bat for each team.

Most Valuable Player (MVP) the player who contributes the most to his or her team's success.

nominate to name as a possible winner.

playoffs a game or series of games to determine a championship or to break a tie.

putout an action that causes a batter or runner on the opposite team to be out.

retire to withdraw from use or service.

rookie a player who is new to the major leagues until he meets certain criteria.

roster an orderly list of people belonging to a professional sports group.

Silver Slugger Award given every year to the best defensive players in MLB.

stolen base when a base runner safely advances to the next base, usually while the pitcher is pitching the ball to home plate.

strike out an out in baseball that results from a batter getting three strikes during a turn at bat.

wild-card a player or team chosen to fill a place in a competition after the regularly qualified players or teams have all been decided.

Online Resources

Booklinks
NONFICTION NETWORK
FREE! ONLINE NONFICTION RESOURCES

To learn more about the Houston Astros, visit **abdobooklinks.com**. These links are routinely monitored and updated to provide the most current information available.

Index